A Theory of Objectivist Parenting

By Roslyn Ross
2015

Table of Contents

1. Contradictions Do Not Exist

Human beings can relate to one another with either mutual respect and freedom or mutual attempts to control and force. Objectivists idealize the former; most of America practices the latter. Though Objectivists are fundamentally against relating to their fellow human beings with various methods of control (bribery, threats, manipulation, slavery), many do not hesitate to relate in that way to the young human beings we temporarily refer to as children. Ayn Rand told me, in her books, that if I ever found a contradiction I needed to check my premises. "Contradictions do not exist," she said.[1]

I spent the last ten years working with children[2] and reading around six hundred books on

---

[1] Francisco d'Anconia says this in *Atlas Shrugged*.
[2] Or the last twenty years if you include the tutoring I did (on and off) from the ages of twelve to twenty-two.

the subject, and I have concluded that Rand is right. Many Objectivist parents base their parenting methods on two incorrect premises: 1) that controlled children grow into free adults and 2) that there simply is no other way to raise good children.

In this book I will explain why it is that controlled children do not tend to grow into free adults. Then I will explain the other way to raise children: my theory of Objectivist parenting, a way of parenting that is entirely consistent with Objectivist ethics.

When I first imagined what parenting would be like in Galt's Gulch, I imagined firm, consistent parents and well-behaved children. I imagined moms similar to the Tiger Mom—less emotional but serious, dedicated, and focused on results. I read a few books on child development, and raising children was so clear, it puzzled me why so many parents struggled with their children. There was one simple rule: reward the behavior you wish to see continue and punish the behavior you wish to see cease.

As a professional executive nanny, using this one rule, for many years, I made children do what their parents thought was best for them, what the children would supposedly thank their parents for later: I trained young children to use the toilet, lose weight, and not bite or hit; I made older children get better grades, lose weight, be more committed athletes, and be more competitive college applicants.

What I learned is that you can manipulate, coerce, require, or train children to do or be pretty much anything—except happy. You *can* give them Prozac, but you cannot force children to be genuinely happy with their lives. Ten years ago this made no sense to me. How could a teenage girl, obese her entire life, not be ecstatic to be thin?

This was similar to something that happened when I was in college. I had just read *Atlas Shrugged* and I gave it to everyone who was important to me. I begged them to read it, but I couldn't make them read it. And even when they did read it, I couldn't make them care. Why is it that the first ten pages of *Atlas Shrugged* were so exhilarating for me and so boring for my friends?

2. Each Creature's Nature

Behaviorism is by far the most common method of control parents use on their children (though many parents are unaware they're using it). Behaviorism is so entrenched in American parenting that I have met more Objectivists who defend it, than Objectivists who say they would never use it on their children. How is this possible when Ayn Rand wrote explicitly about how horrible behaviorism is?

I think that there is a lack of clarity surrounding behaviorist parenting: what it is, what it is not, and what that has to do with Objectivism. Rand said, "The battle of philosophers is a battle for man's mind. If you do not understand their theories, you are vulnerable to the worst among them."[3]

Behaviorism has been around since the late 1800's. It is a psychological theory and methodology

---

[3] *Philosophy: Who Needs It*, chapter 1, "Philosophy: Who Needs It."

that came out of the philosophy of determinism and suffers from the same error: the belief in human existence without consciousness. It can be summarized: humans don't make conscious decisions, they just respond to pain and pleasure. We are victims of our programming and can reprogram ourselves, not through consciousness awareness, but by associating various behaviors with pain and pleasure—which is to say: humans can and should be trained just like rats. Behaviorist methodology is therefore: reward the behavior you wish to see continue and punish the behavior you wish to see cease. The behaviorist purpose is control.

Behaviorist parenting is: influencing a child's behavior using any method of intentional reward (from an approving glance to praise to bribery) or any method of intentional punishment (from a disapproving glance to threats to spanking).

Many Objectivists with whom I have spoken defend the use of behaviorism on children by claiming that children are not rational. This defense does not work logically because it rests on the faulty assumption that behaviorism is designed for or appropriate for irrational human beings when in fact, behaviorism was not designed for any kind of human being as Objectivists understand the term. Objectivists believe that humans are conscious;

behaviorists do not. Behaviorism was designed for a human-animal that will live an unconscious, deterministic existence not very different from that of rats and pigeons, an existence that, according to Rand, does not include reason, mind, values, concepts, thought, judgment, volition, purpose, memory, independence, or self-esteem. [4]

To argue that behaviorism is appropriate for children, from an Objectivist perspective, is to argue that children *do* live an unconscious, deterministic existence, that a child has no form of reason, mind, values, concepts, thought, judgment, volition, purpose, memory, independence, or self-esteem.

The defenders of behaviorism with whom I have argued think it is my job to prove that children are rational and therefore behaviorism is not appropriate. I disagree. It is only my job to point out that children are human, because if, as Objectivists, we subscribe to the belief that humans are conscious, behaviorism is never appropriate. Therefore, defenders of behaviorism must determine *not* at exactly what age a human being's rational faculties are developed enough for him to be called "rational," but at exactly what age children are conscious. If I turn back to Rand, I read:

---

[4] See *Philosophy: Who Needs It*, chapter 13, "The Stimulus and the Response."

When you become aware, implicit in your first sensation are certain axiomatic concepts. And they are what? That you exist, that the outside world exists, and that you are conscious. The baby could not conceptualize this, but it's implicit; without that implication he couldn't be aware of anything.[5]

And from Maria Montessori:

A child starts with nothing and develops his reason, the specific characteristic of man. And he starts along this path even before he can walk upon his own small feet.

This can perhaps be better clarified by an example than by an explanation. I can recall a particularly moving case of a four-week-old infant that had never been out of the house in which he had been born. One day a nurse was holding the child in her arms when his father and his uncle, who happened to live in the same house, were seen together by the child. The two men were of nearly the same height and age. The infant gave a start of surprise and

---

[5] *Introduction to Objectivist Epistemology*, appendix section, "Axiomatic Concepts: Self."

fright at seeing the two men. They were acquainted with our work and set about allaying the child's fears. Still keeping within view of the infant, they separate, one going to the right and the other to the left. The child turned to look at one, and after gazing at him for a while intently, broke into a smile.

But then he suddenly became worried. He turned his head quickly to look at the other. Only after some time did he smile at him. He repeated these actions turning his head from side to side a dozen times and showing alternate signs of concern and relief before he came to realize that there actually were two individuals. These were the only men the child had ever seen. They had both played with him on different occasions, taking him into their arms and speaking affectionately to him. The child had come to realize that there was a being different from his mother, nurse, and the other women of the household, but he had never seen two men together and had obviously concluded that there was only one man. When he was suddenly confronted with two, he became alarmed.

From the chaos that surrounded him, he had isolated a single man and then, when he was confronted with another, he discovered his first error. At the early age of four weeks he had perceived the fallibility of human reason.[6]

And yet I have argued with people who claim that babies are not conscious. But I am not arguing (and neither is Montessori nor Rand) that babies have the same level of functioning of their conscious apparatus that adults do, however, so I will return to the original argument and take the other road.

Let's say that children are not conscious, or at least, not conscious enough to be called human. Does it follow, then, that they should be raised as rodents or circus animals? To advocate the use of behaviorism on pre-conscious human beings is to claim that each creature must act according to its nature—but not from birth. A human can be raised just like a rat because when he reaches maturity he will *magically* transform into a man—a human child doesn't need any different, special, human-child rearing methods to prepare him for being a human adult! To advocate the use of behaviorism on children is to say, "Human-child rearing methods—rat-child rearing methods—why should they be different?"

---

[6] *The Secret of Childhood*, chapter 9, "Intelligence."

I think the "children are not rational" argument is a rather lazy failure to closely examine an obvious contradiction, so I am going to move on to clarifying the issues that will solve the contradiction, but before I do, I want to clarify four things about behaviorism:

An authentic response is not behaviorism. If a baby takes his first steps and his mother responds, "How exciting! You're walking!" that is an authentic expression of her feelings. If she says, "You're walking! Good job!" with the conscious or unconscious belief that her approval will encourage him to walk more, that is behaviorism.

Simple force is not behaviorism. If a child runs into the street and his father saves him, that is not behaviorism. If the boy's father then punishes him—that is.

Not long ago an Objectivist father asked me whether it was still behaviorism if he told his child what he was doing. He thought if he said, "Now son, you understand why I have to punish you, don't you? I have to teach you not to do what you did," then it wasn't behaviorism. Unfortunately, a clear explanation about why you are doing what you are doing, does not change what you are doing.

Lastly, I use the term behaviorism to describe that style of parenting which seeks to control children using external motivators, but it should be noted that the term is no longer in vogue. Behaviorism, rightly, got a bad name, and now when most psychologists discuss the same techniques, and especially if they are going to encourage them, they are simply called "external motivators."

3. The Method Is the Message

Behaviors are actions we take to meet needs, to gain or keep what we value. When the parent controls the child's behavior with rewards and punishments, the parent severs the child's action from the child's values behind the action and makes himself, the parent, the value. Because the parent, not reality, determines when the child feels pain or pleasure, the child's entire orientation changes—from reality to people-as-reality.

In 1958 Nathaniel Branden gave a series of lectures on Objectivism.[7] In one of those lectures he talked about the man who

> lives, not in a universe of facts, but in a universe of people . . . People, not reason, are his tool of survival . . . It is on them that his

---

[7] These lectures were transcribed and printed in Branden's book, *The Vision of Ayn Rand*.

consciousness must focus. It is they who he must understand or please or placate or deceive or maneuver or manipulate or obey. It is his success at this task that becomes the gauge of his fitness to exist.[8]

His metaphysics has been replaced by what Branden calls "social metaphysics."[9]

Because a child's way of relating to the world—his metaphysical orientation—will be largely determined before he is five years old, I think the main cause of social metaphysics, currently, is behaviorist parenting. For example: when a child hits and is put in time out, his parents think they are teaching him to associate hitting with the pain of time out; the child actually learns, not that hitting will lead to pain, but rather, that not pleasing his parents will lead to pain. The child does not need to study, understand, and conquer nature; if he wants to avoid pain, he needs to study, understand, and conquer his parents.

---

[8] *The Vision of Ayn Rand*, chapter 8, "The Psychology of Dependence."

[9] Branden also thoroughly examines social metaphysics in his book *Taking Responsibility: Self-Reliance and the Accountable Life*.

Fast-forward fifteen years. This child raised on behaviorism is now in college. Offer him *Atlas Shrugged* or reality TV. Which one will offer him more information about the reality that he thinks he needs to study, understand, and conquer? And now you know why so many of my friends found *Atlas Shrugged* boring.

In addition to destroying the child's metaphysics, behaviorism also moves the child from being intrinsically motivated (motivated by a self-interested pursuit of values, seeking personal satisfaction derived from self-initiated achievement) to being extrinsically motivated (motivated by external rewards such as fame, grades, and praise, motivation that originates outside the individual).

In his book *Teaching Johnny to Think*, Leonard Peikoff suggests that external motivators can be used for "good" instead of "evil."[10] But extrinsic motivators, by their very nature, require that we suppress our real feelings, desires, and values and replace them with someone else's—extrinsic motivators beget collectivism. It does not matter at all what we are trying to make our children do with extrinsic motivators. We can change the curriculum

---

[10] See chapter 2, "The Teaching of Thinking Methods."

all we want. We can make it a hundred percent Objectivist. Likewise, it won't matter if we spank or use time out or do away with punishments altogether and just focus on rewards—the method is the message.

In *Punished by Rewards: The Trouble with Gold Stars, Incentive Plans, A's, Praise, and Other Bribes*, Alfie Kohn shows that the mechanisms of reward and punishment to control an adult's behavior, only work if the adult was rewarded and punished as a child. Kohn shows that the younger the rewards and punishments start, and the more consistently they are used, the more effective they will be—and the more *necessary* they will be. "We often assume that a system of rewards simply takes advantage of a 'fundamental feature of human character' when it actually '*turns people into* reinforcement-maximizing economic actors.'"[11]

This is not new information. A hundred years ago Maria Montessori wrote, "The prize and the punishment are incentives towards unnatural or forced effort, and therefore we certainly cannot speak

---

[11] Notes section, "Notes to pages 13-17," quoting Barry Schwartz.

of the natural development of the child in connection with them."[12]

Behaviorist parents say, "You hit Jenny. You are bad. What you should be feeling is shame. Go stand in the corner and feel shame. You may feel better when I say so." Or, "You didn't do your homework. You don't know what's best for you, and I do. I must make you do what is best for you. Only the goals I deem rational are worth pursuing. You can be rational . . . by agreeing with me!"

Parents who use rewards and punishments are attempting to control their child's perceptions of reality, so that the child will make the decisions the parents want him to make. The result for the child is confusion, insecurity in his own ability to interpret reality, and massive repression. All of these things get in the way of rational thought and prevent the integration of the child's emotional brain with his developing rational faculty.

Ayn Rand wrote that "the field of extrospection is based on two cardinal questions: 'What do I know?' and 'How do I know it?' In the

---

[12] Quoted in Angeline Lillard, *Montessori: The Science Behind the Genius*, chapter 5, "Extrinsic Rewards and Motivation."

field of introspection, the questions are: 'What do I feel?' and 'Why do I feel it?'"[13]

It is in the contemplation of, the thinking about, the analyzing and understanding of the answers to these questions that we teach our children to use their brains to the best of their abilities; it is through these questions that we help our children develop an integrated mind, an understanding of why they feel what they feel about what they know.

Extrinsic controls prevent these questions from being asked. It sounds like this: "What do I feel and why? Who cares, a candy bar will fix it!" With babies it sounds like this: "What do you feel and why? Who cares, shhhhhhut up. Shhhhhhh." Or with children: "What do you feel and why? Who cares, go to your room until you can calm down and talk to me like a normal person."

Parents think they are teaching their children self-control, but really, they are teaching emotional repression: "You may not feel that. You may not talk to me until you have repressed what you are feeling." Aletha J. Solter writes:

The repression of crying during infancy is so pervasive that most babies have well-

---

[13] *Philosophy: Who Needs It*, chapter 2, "Philosophical Detection."

established control patterns by the time they are six months old. These behaviors serve the purpose of repressing strong emotions. Common Control patterns in babies include thumb sucking or pacifier sucking, frequent demands to nurse for comfort rather than hunger, and attachment to an object such as a special blanket or teddy bear.[14]

Other common ways young children stop themselves from crying include hyperactivity, self-rocking, head-banging, and distractions such as entertainment.

By the time they are ready for preschool, teachers expect children to have learned somewhat to "control" their emotions. But what is meant by "control" is actually repression. The emotional stress of repression often manifests as facial ticks, considered "normal" in three to five-year-olds. Nathaniel Branden wrote:

No one can be integrated, no one can function harmoniously, no one can think clearly and effectively about the deep issues of life who is

---

[14] *Tears and Tantrums: What To Do When Babies and Children Cry*, part II, "How Crying is Repressed in Babies: The Origin of Control Patterns."

oblivious to the internal signals, manifested as feelings and emotions, rising from within the organism . . . Most of us have been encouraged to deny and repress who we are, to disown our feelings, to disown important aspects of the self, almost from the day we were born. [15]

And:

Fear and pain should be treated as signals not to close our eyes but to open them wider, not to look away but to look more attentively.[16]

Extrinsic controls teach children to ignore the emotional information they receive from their own minds. The result is that children often fail to develop an intrinsic self (i.e. a real self) at all. Instead they adopt an extrinsic, unreal self.

Hence the epidemic of twenty-two-year-olds today[17] who have no idea what they enjoy doing just for the sake of doing it. They are motivated by

---

[15] *The Vision of Ayn Rand*, "Epilogue: The Benefits and Hazards of the Philosophy of Ayn Rand."
[16] *The Six Pillars of Self-Esteem*, chapter 6, "The Practice of Living Consciously."
[17] And me, ten years ago.

money, prestige, winning, approval, and above all, by pats on the head for being Good Boys and Girls. They use behaviorism on themselves: they promise themselves a new outfit if they just lose ten pounds or a week of self-loathing if they don't.[18]

Even if they find Objectivism, they often don't know how to selfishly and righteously be themselves; instead, they seek to be Good Little Objectivists. In *The Six Pillars of Self-Esteem* Nathaniel Branden wrote about how many Good Little Objectivists he saw in his practice, people who missed the point—people who were trained from birth to miss the point. He wrote of a client:

> We discovered that what he had always wanted to be was a research scientist but that he had abandoned that desire in deference to his parents, who pushed him toward a career in business. Not only was he unable to feel more than the most superficial kind of pride in his accomplishments but he was wounded in his self-esteem . . . He had surrendered his mind and values to the wishes of others . . .

---

[18] See Doris Fromberg and Doris Bergen, *Play From Birth to Twelve: Contexts, Perspectives, and Meanings*, chapter 7, "Play in the Context of Life-Span Human Development."

We sometimes hear people say, "I have accomplished so much. Why don't I feel more proud of myself?" . . . It can be useful to ask, "Who *chose* your goals? You, or the voice of some 'significant other' inside you?"[19]

And in *The Vision of Ayn Rand* he wrote:

When admirers of Ayn Rand seek my services professionally, they often come with the secret hope, rarely acknowledged in words, that with Nathaniel Branden they will at last become the masters of repression needed to fulfill the dream of becoming an ideal Objectivist . . . I have known many men and women who, in the name of lofty beliefs, crucify their bodies, crucify their feelings, and crucify their emotional lives, in order to live up to that which they call their values. Just like the followers of one religion or another who, absorbed in some particular vision of what they think human beings can be or should be, they leave the human beings they actually are

---

[19] Chapter 2, "The Meaning of Self-Esteem."

in a very bad place: a place of neglect and even damnation.[20]

Ayn Rand said, "It is the hardest thing in the world—to do what we want."[21] Extrinsic controls make it the hardest thing in the world to even know what we want.

This is why it seems to high school teachers that extrinsic motivators simply must be used. Children's intrinsic motivation has been shown to decline every year over the course of traditional schooling. By the time they are in high school, they rarely display any intrinsic motivation whatsoever.[22]

---

[20] "Epilogue: The Benefits and Hazards of the Philosophy of Ayn Rand."

[21] Peter Keating has this realization in *The Fountainhead*.

[22] See Angeline Lillard, *Montessori: The Science Behind the Genius*, chapter 5, "Extrinsic Rewards and Motivation." Note that "having no intrinsic motivation whatsoever" means having no self, having no internal values, no internal direction; it means being easily controlled, since the only thing that propels you to act is what comes from outside of yourself, what other people can give you. This is a scientifically documented result of our education system—and there is considerable evidence to suggest that it was no accident; see Charlotte Thomson Iserbyt's *The Deliberate Dumbing Down of*

Behaviorism creates the problem for which behaviorism is the only solution.

And so behaviorism seems to work! Not on an intrinsic or authentic level, but on a "my human-rodent pet is behaving in a way that pleases me" level. This is why science shows that behaviorism will only ever "work" in the short term and will backfire in the long term. For example, children rewarded for playing with markers will play with them more . . . as long as the rewards keep coming, and then they will play with them significantly less than the non-rewarded children.[23] What's the best way to make your child dislike doing something he already enjoyed? Reward him for doing it.

Repeated experiments done on how to best impose the value of altruism[24] on young children have shown that children rewarded for altruistic behaviors will only behave altruistically as long as the adult is there to reward them. Then they will behave less

---

America: A Chronological Paper Trail, and John Gatto's Dumbing Us Down: The Hidden Curriculum of Compulsory Schooling.
[23] See Angeline Lillard, Montessori: The Science Behind the Genius, chapter 5, "Extrinsic Rewards and Motivation."
[24] Part of the definition of "prosocial behavior," the term used in most studies.

altruistically when the adult isn't there.[25] This is why extrinsically motivated adults find that, like children, they are only "good" when someone is watching.[26]

This is another impulse of collectivism: people want someone to make them do what they can't make themselves do. They say they vote for a nanny state to keep all the "bad people" under control, but subconsciously they want a nanny for themselves. This is also one of the impulses of some religions: if you can only be good when someone else is watching, they have a solution for you.

This is what I didn't understand ten years ago: you can get children to do or be pretty much anything, but goals achieved through external motivators will not make the child happy.

---

[25] See Alfie Kohn, *Punished by Rewards: The Trouble with Gold Stars, Incentive Plans, A's, Praise, and Other Bribes*, chapter 6, "The Praise Problem."
[26] Kohn also shows that rewards only seem to work (or work in the short run) on adults as well. When rewards are used in the workplace, productivity will soar for three to six months, and then employees will report a drop in job satisfaction, and productivity will fall. Since many companies focus on the next quarter spike rather than long-term slow-and-steady growth, this fact is often ignored (see chapter 10, "Thank God It's Monday: The Roots of Motivation in the Workplace").

4. For Their Own Good

Being in control of one's children, playing the part of the controller, a serene, loving dictator, it makes parenting seem so easy—in our heads. In reality the parent is controlled by his role that requires him to be "in control." He has to mete out a punishment or reward based on the behavior of his child and is then further controlled by how his child responds to his controls.

Our tendencies, when we are in controlling relationships, have a lot in common with social metaphysics:

- We can't be present with our child in this moment if we are busy thinking of ways to get him to do what we want him to do and monitoring whether what we are doing is working. This limits our ability to enjoy our relationships with our children, to be consciously aware of them, to connect.

- We can't allow ourselves to be visible to people we are trying to control; that would be "showing our cards"; they would know our weaknesses, and then they might "win." This leads to a loss of integrity since we are not being honest, so we will lie more, this time to ourselves. We will tell ourselves that we do not have to be honest because the people we are trying to control don't merit our honesty.

- When we are controlling other people, we cannot allow ourselves to truly see them, because to do so, we would have to be aware of the pain and suffering we are inflicting on them. So our tendency is to see their feelings as not real—that's not real pain children suffer when they cry. (This is why controlling relationships can so easily lead to evil, because our tendency will be to fail to see the person we are trying to control as a person. As with slaves, women, "savages", or "heathens"—we transform our adversary into something that needs to be controlled: "Oh, children, they're irrational, like rats; they feel safer when you control them; they need it.")

- Even if we do see the feelings of those we control as real, we convince ourselves their pain is okay; it's for their own good. Maria Montessori wrote:

One of the most remarkable
camouflages is the hypocrisy with
which an adult treats a child. An adult
sacrifices a child's needs to his own,
but he refuses to recognize the fact,
since this would be intolerable. He
persuades himself that he is exercising
a natural right and acting for the future
good of the child. When the child
defends himself, the adult does not
advert to what is really happening but
judges whatever the child does to save
himself as disobedience and the result
of evil tendencies.[27] The feeble voice
of truth and justice within the adult
grows weak and is replaced by the
false conviction that one is acting
prudently, according to one's right and
duty, and so forth.[28]

- In controlling relationships, the controller has
  a tendency to feel that he has not chosen to be
  in a relationship with those he is controlling.
  Rather, he sees himself as responsible for

[27] Note that Objectivists who do this use the word
"irrational" instead of "evil."
[28] *The Secret of Childhood*, chapter 23, "Deviations."

them, for their welfare, for their souls. It's hard to enjoy a relationship that is actually a duty.

- Since the parents don't see children as real people with whom they can connect, they often end up putting on a show. For example, a man might play the role of Good Father by mowing the lawn, taking out the trash, reading to the kids, doing bath time, helping his wife with the dishes, getting the highest paying job he can, and working his tail off. At first he will pat himself on the back as he thinks, "I am such a Good Father!" But, after a while, he will start to feel like being a Good Father is a huge obligation, a chore, a long list of things to do. It won't be fun anymore. And if he could admit it to himself, he might find that he resents his wife and children, whom he sees as his slave drivers. But it's not them; it's the role. It's the lack of conscious awareness with which he is living his life.

- When we are playing roles we have a tendency not to take responsibility for our choices. For example, someone playing the role of "soldier" or "policeman" may not very closely examine what he is doing or even feel responsible for the morality of his choices if he sees it as part of his role, as "just doing his job."

- Controlling relationships have a tendency to be exhausting. It takes a lot of energy to be inauthentic, to be actors, to do what we believe we "should" do to be Good Moms and Dads, to suppress our true selves and how we really feel about reading the same book a hundred times.

We often take on roles and follow scripts without even meaning to. Henry David Thoreau's *Walden* is my favorite example of this. Most people know the story: Thoreau built a cabin in the woods to "discover himself" and what life was all about for him. He did it even though his neighbors thought he was a little weird. What he learned and wrote about is that the secret of life is knowing (or finding) your authentic, intrinsic self, and setting your own goals despite society's judgments. But what many people take away from *Walden* is that the secret to life is leaving society and living in a cabin in the woods. This is a misunderstanding. We should advance confidently in the direction of *our own* dreams.

Whether we take on roles accidentally or whether roles are designed by those in power and handed to the masses for specific purposes, controlling the roles and scripts of a society is a great way to direct the masses without them knowing it.

One of my favorite professors at Wesleyan University, Kach Tololyan, clarified this idea for me when he said: "Those who create 'normal' rule the world." Whether it's: "this is what a nursery looks like," "this is what an education looks like," "this is what an expertise in children looks like," or "this is what a good parent looks like," our society's roles and scripts have tremendous power over us.

For more than a hundred years the parenting role, perhaps the most important script to control, has been handed to us by academia, by the same people who teach Keynesian economics and Kantian philosophy.[29] Perhaps, like me, you were trained from birth to accept academia as your church; perhaps you think it's a different academia from the one Ayn Rand was writing about when she wrote:

It is the *Educational Establishment* that determines the ideas of a nation. It is your

---

[29] To really horrify yourself read *Dare the School Build a New Social Order, The Leipzig Connection, The Change Agent's Guide to Innovation in Education, Deschooling Society, The Underground History of American Education*, and *The Deliberate Dumbing Down of America*.

professors' ideas that have ruled the world for the past fifty years or longer, with a growing spread of devastation, not improvement.[30]

Or when she wrote:

What chance would a beginner, a nonconformist, an opponent of behaviorism, have against the entrenched power of a clique supported by government funds? This is not a free marketplace of ideas any longer . . . Today's culture is ruled by intellectual pressure groups which have become intellectual monopolies backed, like all monopolies, by the government's gun and the money of the victims.[31]

Or when she wrote:

Of any one group involved, it is not the comprachicos who are the guiltiest, it is the parents—particularly the educated ones who could afford to send their children to

---

[30] *Return of the Primitive: The Anti-Industrial Revolution,* "The Comprachicos."
[31] *Philosophy: Who Needs It*, chapter 13, "The Stimulus and the Response."

Progressive nursery schools. Such parents would do anything for their children, except give a moment's thought or an hour's critical inquiry into the nature of the educational institutions selected. [32]

A respectful relationship *requires* presence, self-awareness, visibility, integrity, honesty, interacting with reality—internal as well as external. There cannot be a script for reality, because every moment that ever happens has never happened before.

I recommend that Objectivist parents question every aspect of the Good Parent script that has been implanted in their brains and that they ask themselves: To what extent do I base my success as a parent on my ability to control my child? Is there a

---

[32] *Return of the Primitive: The Anti-Industrial Revolution*, "The Comprachicos." Also, some Objectivists put their children into Montessori schools but never actually read her books, so they are unaware that the school that they have chosen is more progressive than Montessori. Six tips it's not authentic Montessori: 1) multi-colored work objects; 2) work periods of less than three hours; 3) three-year-olds separated from six-year-olds; 4) fantasy fiction books offered to the kids; 5) any form of extrinsic reward, including praise; 6) teachers wandering the room.

way to control my child (or anyone), without practicing social metaphysics?

5. The Last Consequence

Every conqueror since antiquity has known that he does not have to worry about those he has conquered, he just has to take over how their children are raised. Ayn Rand mentioned this as well. She wrote, "'Give me a child for the first seven years . . . and you may do what you like with him afterwards' . . . is true of most children, with rare, heroically independent exceptions." [33]

Most people interpret this statement to mean that humans are creatures of habit who live unconscious lives determined by their childhood. For an Objectivist, this statement means that it must be possible to destroy a person's mind so successfully in

---

[33] *Return of the Primitive: The Anti-Industrial Revolution*, "The Comprachicos."

childhood that he is rendered unconscious (at least morally) for the rest of his life.[34]

I explained how that happens in previous chapters; what I want to add now is that when we, as parents, combine the mind destruction of external motivators with playing the role of a warmly authoritative benevolent dictator to our children, we create in our children a habit of subjugation that only "heroically independent exceptions" will escape.

External motivators will always lead to mind-destruction as the method is the message, but even without external motivators playing a role will also always cause problems, because whatever role the parent is playing, he is modeling unconsciousness, inauthenticity, and dishonesty.

It should not surprise Objectivists that in a culture where we benevolently dictate to our children, our government benevolently dictates to us. Ayn Rand said, "Politics is the last consequence, the practical implementation, of the fundamental (metaphysical-epistemological-ethical) ideas that dominate a given nation's culture. You cannot fight

---

[34] A different way to say this is: Unable to reach a level of abstraction in which he comes to moral conclusions on his own.

or change the consequences without fighting and changing the cause."[35]

If Objectivists don't want their government to be a benevolent dictatorship, their households cannot be benevolent dictatorships. If Objectivists want to live in a society like Galt's Gulch—their households must be its model. It is possible that a lack of focus on parenting is the biggest flaw in the Objectivist movement.

Behaviorist parenting, the default method of parenting in our culture, fosters the turning of our children into collectivists and non-people. It demands that parents relinquish their personhood and become role-playing puppets (more non-people).[36] And it leads to the creation of a collectivist society. It has no place in an Objectivist household.

---

[35] *Philosophy: Who Needs It,* chapter 17, "What Can One Do."

[36] Behaviorism is not the *only* way children are turned into collectivists; see Ayn Rand's essay, "The Comprachicos" and Leonard Peikoff's *Teaching Johnny to Think*.

6. Objectivist Parenting

Human beings can relate to one another with either mutual respect and freedom or mutual attempts to control and force. Though Objectivists idealize the former, we were all raised with the latter. This makes it hard, even for us, to imagine any other way to parent.

For example, William R Thomas wrote, "Children regularly have to be restrained from doing what they want to do and forced to do something else. They have to be put to bed and made to wash."[37]

We have been offered this dichotomy our entire lives: Either we control our children, or they live lives of chaos. Either we make our kids go to bed and wash, or they won't. If that were the choice, I

---

[37] William R Thomas, "The Foundations of Criminal Child Welfare Law in a Rights-Based Political System."

would agree with Thomas. But that choice is a trick. That is not the choice.

Similarly, Nathaniel Branden[38] advises parents to be warm but authoritative and cites a scientific study that was done in which four types of parents were studied—warmly authoritative, coldly authoritative, warmly permissive, and coldly permissive.[39] Again, if those *are* the only choices, then by all means, I agree that parents should be warmly authoritative. But again, the choice is a trick. What we are being offered is a false dichotomy, a dichotomy that only makes sense as long as we are

---

[38] Nathaniel Branden is one of the "giants on whose shoulders I stand," and I strongly recommend every book he has written.

[39] Branden also misses that this study (and many others, if not most) recommends "warmly authoritative" parenting because that type of parenting results in children who are "well-adjusted," meaning "socially responsible, friendly, cooperative, and altruistic." I would be much more interested in a study that determined the style of parenting that resulted in children with the virtues of rationality, integrity, honesty, productivity, independence, justice, and pride. I agree with Rand that, "The indoctrination of children with a mob spirit—under the category of 'social adjustment'—is conducted openly and explicitly." And I will add, as if it were a good thing. See *Return of the Primitive: The Anti-Industrial Revolution*, "The Comprachicos."

stuck in what I call the "operating system of control and force."

If a study were done on whether people prefer to exploit or be exploited in trade, Objectivists would see right through it. They would explain the operating system of freedom and respect in which they trade value for value, in which they would neither exploit nor be exploited in a trade.

But this explanation would be incomprehensible to those who operate in the system of control, in which employers and employees are always adversaries trying to take advantage of one another. No matter how hard Objectivists try to explain that trade can be win-win, people who operate in the system of control can only see things on the spectrum of control—either you are exploiting me, or I am exploiting you; either I sacrifice myself to others, or they sacrifice themselves to me.

When my son was two years old people kept asking me, "Is he defiant yet?" This is a question that would only make sense to someone who operates in the system of control. I don't operate there, so I would say something like, "To be defiant, one must have someone to defy. There must be a ruler and a subject, someone in control and someone being controlled. I don't relate to my son in that way."

"Ah," the people would reply, smiling sadly at me, "you're permissive. You just let your son do whatever he wants!" If I am not authoritative, I must be permissive; if I'm not the master, I must be the slave. This is the same false dichotomy. It's as if there are two operating systems, and to live in one negates the existence of the other. William Glasser wrote:

> The vast majority of family unhappiness is the result of well-intentioned parents trying to make children do what they don't want to do . . .
>
> Few of us are prepared to accept that it is our attempts to control that destroys the only thing we have with our children that gives us some control[40] over them, our relationship.[41]

Thomas Gordon said the same thing: "The more you use power to try to control people, the less real influence you have on their lives."[42]

---

[40] I think "influence" would have been a better choice of word here.

[41] *Choice Theory: A New Psychology of Personal Freedom,* chapter 9, "Trust and Your Family."

[42] Quoted in Alfie Kohn, *Punished by Rewards: The Trouble with Gold Stars, Incentive Plans, A's, Praise, and Other Bribes,* chapter 9, "Bribes for Behaving:

The choice isn't control or chaos. The choice, in human relationships, does not change based on the age of the people involved. The choice is: mutual respect or mutual attempts to control. Mutual respect is the other way to parent.

In my relationship with my son, I see myself as an ambassador for this fabulous place I live, Galt's Gulch, and I see my son as a distinguished visitor from a far-off land who does not understand my customs. It is my goal to help him thrive in my land, but not at the point of a gun. Instead, I strive to respect him, to understand his strange culture, and to show him how to respect me in my strange culture. When we run into a situation in which one of us is doing something that bothers the other—perhaps he wants to throw beans on the floor, and I don't want him to, or I want to leave the park, and he doesn't want to—I think some version of: "This is what I want; this is what my distinguished houseguest wants; what can we do to get both of our needs met in this situation?"

Thinking about our relationship in this way means we make no attempts to control or manipulate one another; there is no fear, resentment, obfuscation, or subterfuge. There is no "power struggle," just two

Why Behaviorism Doesn't Help Children Become Good People."

people relating to one another with presence, visibility, accurate information, honesty, and integrity.

Relating to children in this way can be extremely difficult at first as we must learn a way of relating to children for which we have had no models, a way of relating to children that contradicts everything we have been socialized to believe.

The good news is that if we take the time to learn this way of relating to children, it makes parenting much easier in the long run. Thomas Gordon wrote a book advocating similar parenting methods to mine. He wrote of families parenting in this way that, "The most significant outcome . . . and one that I had not expected, is . . . conflicts simply do not come up very often."[43]

This has been my experience. I have never made my son go to bed or wash, yet he does both of those things every day (and if he didn't want to one day, it would not be an issue). Rue Kream wrote:

You say you 'have to' pick him up and take him [to the bath]. I like to question my have

---

[43] *Parent Effectiveness Training: The Proven Program for Raising Responsible Children,* chapter 12, "Parents' Fears and Concerns about the "No-Lose" Method."

to-s, especially when they are leading to unhappiness for my children. What would happen if you didn't pick him up and take him? What would happen if he didn't take a bath that night? What message is he getting from being picked up and put somewhere he doesn't want to be? Is it truly more important that he take a bath than it is for the two of you to build a respectful relationship?[44]

And:

It is usually assumed that children who aren't made to obey their parents will grow to be unruly, disrespectful, and 'out of control.' Nothing could be further from the truth. Children who are treated with respect are respectful of others . . . A family where parents and children are allies is a peaceful family.[45]

And:

---

[44] *Parenting A Free Child: An Unschooled Life*, question 28, "If I want my son to take a bath . . ."
[45] *Parenting A Free Child: An Unschooled Life*, question 40, "What about the idea that we should remember who the parent is . . ."

Children who know that they are truly free to make their own decisions make responsible, carefully considered choices.[46]

---

[46] *Parenting A Free Child: An Unschooled Life,* question 41, "Isn't it a parent's duty. . ."

7. Concrete Examples

I think the best way to clarify these ideas is with concrete examples. I will start with a newborn baby because some people can imagine how they would treat older children with respect, but it is very hard for them to understand how one could show respect to a lump.

These scenarios involve real interactions I had with my son, or with those children for whom I cared, and were inspired by the books listed in the Appendix.

Scenario 1: A newborn baby and how he is fed

The Standard American Mom sees it as her job to get food into her baby, so she brings her baby to her breast, tickles his cheek to trigger his mouth-opening reflex, and puts her breast in his mouth.

My proposed Objectivist Mom does not think it would be respectful to just put something in someone's mouth, even a quadriplegic's. She brings her baby to her breast so that her nipple is near his nose and mouth and he can smell what she is offering. If he wants to nurse, he can open his mouth and do so.[47]

Scenario 2: A newborn baby and when he is fed

The Standard American Mom believes that to be a Good Mom she is supposed to feed her baby every two hours. She has a handy little device that goes off every two hours, so she knows it's time to feed the baby. If he acts hungry before the two hours is up, she distracts him so that he learns to wait two hours.

The Objectivist Mom thinks refusing to feed her distinguished visitor, when she is capable of accommodating him, is disrespectful, so she feeds her baby when he's hungry. Maybe it's been one hour; maybe it's been three.

---

[47] I am not making the claim that nursing is easy, effortless, and natural; nursing is a "lost art," and I strongly recommend lactation consultants.

Assuming these are interaction patterns, and not single events, here is an analysis of what has been learned:

The Objectivist Baby is responsible for his eating: his mind is learning to connect the sensation of hunger with the solution—food. He must learn to recognize the sensation of hunger and communicate it to his mother. He has found a benevolent universe and already sees himself as a capable actor in it.

The Standard American Baby has food shoved into his mouth whether he wants it or not, and it will be done when the clock says, whether he is hungry or not. In his mind, the connection between hunger and food has not been made. Likewise he has learned nothing about communication or self-assertion, except that there is no point since it doesn't work. This baby will oscillate between feelings of frustration and anger as he fails repeatedly to communicate to his mother, and passive resignation as he tries to accept the universe that he has found.

For the moms: the Objectivist Mom is getting in tune with her baby. The Standard American Mom is getting in tune with her alarm clock—and whether she means to or not—showing her baby who is in control. It's not him. It's also not her. It's the alarm clock and the script it represents. She is just doing what she has been told.

A Theory of Objectivist Parenting

Scenario 3: A teething one-year-old bites his mom while nursing

The Standard American Mom believes it is her job to teach her child not to bite people. When he bites her she gives him a disapproving look, and says "Bad boy! No Biting!" Then she picks him up and puts him in time out for one minute, because that's how long time outs are when you are one year old.

The Objectivist Mom first responds authentically to what happened. She says, "Ow! You hurt me!" She looks her baby in the eye, communicating her pain, and says, "Please don't bite me, but," and she looks around and grabs a nearby doll, "you want to bite. Here is something you can bite. It won't hurt the doll."

Analysis:

The Standard American Baby has learned that he is bad, that his desire—to bite—is bad. He has learned that some people get to control others, that he is not the one in control, and that he has to please those who are in control or he will suffer. He has learned that not only should he not want what he wants, trying to get what he wants could lead to pain.

The Objectivist Baby has learned that it is okay for him to want what he wants. He wants to bite, and that's fine. There's nothing wrong with him; there's no shame. On the contrary his mother supports his desire to learn what he wants to learn, and she will help him get those needs met in a way that also works for her.

Scenario 4: Eating dinner with a four-year-old

The Standard American Mom believes it is her job to get food into her child, especially vegetables. In order to accomplish this goal she does a variety of things: begging him to take one more bite, bribing him with desert, making macaroni and cheese every night because he won't eat anything else, and making vegetable purees and sneaking them into his macaroni and cheese.

The Objectivist Mom knows she wants to eat dinner and shares whatever she makes for herself with her child, just as she has since he was a baby. Tonight she makes bratwurst, sauerkraut, and mashed potatoes. What her child decides to do at this point is his business. She talks to him during dinner; she never even looks at his plate.

Analysis:

The Standard American Child has learned that he has to eat whether he is hungry or not. He has been taught not to listen to his body, to ignore his own perceptions of reality. He has been taught that sometimes you have to be sneaky to make people do what you want. He has learned that he does have some power in his relationship with his mom—the power to refuse food. He enjoys using that to get a little revenge on her.

The Objectivist Child has been in charge of his eating since he was a baby. He has been eating whatever his mom makes since he was a baby. Sometime he eats it, sometimes he doesn't. Especially if it's a new food, sometimes he doesn't even taste it. He eats vegetables when he wants to, but there has never been any pressure or guilt. He has no guilt associated with food! Eating is all his deal, his responsibility. He has learned that he is capable of taking care of himself in this way. He has learned to trust his body to tell him how much to eat, that his perceptions of reality are valid. He knows that his body belongs to him.

When I started working with children I behaved exactly as the Standard American Mom in these scenarios. Today, I can't help but feel a deep sadness at what I did not know. My heart goes out to any reader who is feeling similarly.

8. No Forbidden Knowledge

I spent many years working with children and behaving exactly as the Standard American Mom does in the last chapter. By the time my son was born I was behaving exactly as the Objectivist Mom does. Which is to say: I have raised, or helped to raise, children in both ways, and I cannot state strongly enough how much more satisfying it is to raise children in the operating system of respect.

For me, the easiest part of moving into the system of respect was relating to my son as a foreign dignitary. The hardest part was learning how to deal with my son's strong emotions.

All children (and adults) experience very strong emotions. Communicating in a respectful way with children (and adults) who are feeling strong emotions is a learned skill. Failing to learn this skill is the main reason why many parents who want to have respectful relationships with their children revert to various control tactics. In fact, I don't think having a mutually respectful relationship with children is even possible if the adult does not learn this skill.

Here is the wonderful problem with my parenting theory: we cannot give our children what we don't have—psychological economics! That means that this skill we must learn starts with us, the adults. It starts with how we think about our own strong emotions.

American socialization involves many ideas about emotions that are extremely destructive and inconsistent with Objectivism. This chapter will focus on one of them—the idea of "emotional control." Since most people begin with the assumption that emotions are primary, they seek ways to control and influence their emotional states. But our emotions let us know how we are doing; they help point us in the right direction; they let us know what is working and what needs our attention. Our strong emotions tell us: pay attention to this! If we listen, our emotions can be great aids in the pursuit of our values. But attempting to manipulate them, like attempting to command what we see or hear, is just refusing to acknowledge reality. It doesn't change reality and does not serve us. Nathaniel Branden writes:

Mental health does not require total
omniscience about the contents and operation
of one's subconscious, just as it does not
require total omniscience about the external
world . . . But it does require the total absence,
on the conscious and subconscious level, of
any premise forbidding knowledge. It requires
that man place no value above awareness,
which means: no value above the ability to
perceive, the ability to be conscious.[48]

Earlier in this book I explained that a
controlling approach to raising children creates a
great deal of emotional repression—i.e., the
forbidding of knowledge. The parenting in Galt's
Gulch must yield the opposite: no repressions, no
forbidden knowledge—external or internal.

This is hard to picture because most of us
were raised to believe that we are good when we keep
ourselves "under control" and bad when we "lose
control." When we lose control we must, as quickly
as possible, get ourselves back under control, often by
hiding, alone and ashamed, until our strong feelings
have subsided, perhaps with the help of alcohol, food,

---

[48] *The Vision of Ayn Rand*, chapter 2, "What is
Reason?"

sex, pharmaceuticals, television, computer games, excessive sleep or work, etc.

But just like our children, we're not actually getting "in control," so much as we are repressing our feelings. When I first pictured what unrepressed feelings might look like, I imagined a horror show of people freaking out irrationally all the time. Then I realized that I was still thinking in the operating system of control.

It's the same false dichotomy as before, only this time the threat is within: Either you control your emotions or they control you; either you are the master of your emotions, or you are their slave. I would like to propose that, again, this is not the choice.

The actual choice, when it comes to our emotions, our inner reality, is not between control and chaos, but again between control and respect. The path to emotional awareness starts with treating emotions with respect. The choice is to know what we feel or not to know what we feel: consciousness or unconsciousness. Ayn Rand said:

> If men identified introspectively their inner states one tenth as correctly as they identify their objective reality, we would be a race of ideal giants. I ascribe ninety-five percent or

more of all psychological trouble and personal tragedies to the fact that in the realm of introspection . . . men are not only not taught to introspect, they are actively discouraged from engaging in introspection, and yet their lives depend on it.[49]

Introspection means constantly asking the questions, "What do I feel?" and "Why do I feel it?" and having the emotional skills to answer these questions with a great deal of conscious awareness. To quickly summarize a very complex process, this means, according to Nathaniel Branden:

One: we must not repress. We cannot examine a value we are not willing to realize we have. We cannot get a need met, if we don't know what we need. We must know what we know. We must acknowledge what we are feeling—whatever we are feeling: the desire to hit our child, the desire to kick a dog, etc.

If we judge an emotion as bad or undesirable, we will automatically repress it, so it is essential that the acknowledgement is non-judgmental and respectful.

---

[49] Ayn Rand, *Introduction to Objectivist Epistomology: Expanded Second Edition,* appendix section, "Concepts of Consciousness."

Acknowledging that one is experiencing the emotion will stop the repression. That is the goal. (This is why music or movies can help us sometimes. We were repressing something, and then a certain song comes on. It helps to bring our feelings to the surface, and we cry.)

Two: we must feel what we are feeling. Some psychological theories recommend saying, "I'm angry," and then watching the anger as if it is not our anger. These theories teach us to not take responsibility for our feelings. Other popular theories tell us to acknowledge our negative feelings, so as not to repress them, but then to find something more positive to focus on. "What you focus on expands," they say—so don't focus on your negative emotions. But if we don't focus on them, we cannot learn anything from them.

Nathaniel Branden advises us to go into our emotions and invite them into our conscious awareness. This step is crucial because this is how we gather as much information as possible. Emotions must be felt all the way because surface feelings are often misleading.

For example, I know that when I feel depressed, if I bring that depression into my conscious awareness and allow myself to feel it, I usually find that I am just tired. If I didn't take a minute to feel the depression, I would mistakenly think that depression was the problem rather than exhaustion.

Branden wrote:

> Learning the art of relating to emotions in this way is not easy. Virtually everyone initially encounters difficulties. Therapy clients comment on their emotions, they "explain" their emotions, they apologize for their emotions, they speculate as to the historical origins of their emotions—and of course they reproach and even ridicule themselves for their emotions—but they find it extraordinarily difficult to simply let themselves *feel* their emotions . . . If we are willing to stay fully present in our emotions without denial or disowning, the result typically is not the collapse of reason but the emergence of a more lucid awareness. In other words, feel deeply to think clearly.[50]

Three: we must reflect. Some psychological theories instruct us to ride the wave of an emotion;

---

[50] *The Art of Living Consciously*, chapter 5, "Self-Awareness: Examining Our Inner World."

that's all we have to do, since we are just victims of waves of emotion that just happen to wash over us. And though simply experiencing an emotion can be enough in some circumstances, emotions are not causeless, and they should be examined.

For example: I acknowledged my feelings of depression; I realized I was really feeling exhaustion. Now, rather than shrug, have a cup of coffee, and go on with my day, I examine the decisions I made that led to my feelings of exhaustion; I become more aware of my limits, and take action to plan my schedule more appropriately. Then I must examine the depression. What abstract rule or judgment led me to mistake exhaustion for depression? In this particular case, I feel deeply ashamed of my own exhaustion and don't want to admit my limits—I would rather be depressed than admit that I am tired. Deep down, I believe depression is less shameful than resting. This is important information for me to bring into my conscious awareness! Only with awareness of my inaccurate abstractions can I change them.

Our children will only be able to acknowledge, feel, and examine their uncomfortable feelings if we can model this for them and guide them from day one.

Recall scenario 2 from the last chapter concerning when to feed a baby. When the Objectivist Mom can accommodate her hungry baby, she does. But sometimes she cannot accommodate her baby. Perhaps her baby communicates to her that he is hungry, but she is in the middle of cooking dinner. Or perhaps she is driving home, and it would be dangerous to pull over.

At these times the Objectivist Mom tells her baby honestly that she knows what he wants, but she cannot accommodate him. She does not attempt to distract him from his disappointed feelings, but rather, she listens empathetically to him while he expresses his disappointment. Her baby learns that sometimes his actions will not yield what he wants; sometimes he will feel disappointment — and that's *okay*.

Compare this to what the Standard American Baby learns: Whenever he is upset, his mother distracts him from how he feels, sometimes with bouncing motions and sometimes by shoving something shiny in his face. The Standard American Baby has gotten the message that the emotion he was expressing is *not okay,* and when he feels that he should distract himself. As he gets older he will likely continue to distract himself with television, computer games, pharmaceuticals, work, sugar, alcohol, sex, or some other drug that enables him to maintain a façade of "control."

9. The Heroic Parents of Galt's Gulch

If we do not get to be warmly authoritative benevolent dictators to our children, but we absolutely do want to influence what kind of people they become, our only option is to have an awesome, present, respectful relationship with our children, and model how to live an awesome life.

This is actually a far more effective way to parent because, according to Nathaniel Branden, regardless of what we think we're teaching with all our force and control, "We teach what we are."[51]

The only way to raise a hero is to be one. So instead of obsessing over our children and trying to control them, trying to make them be the person we dream they could be, the best way to parent is to focus on ourselves and make ourselves the person we dream of being. Instead of, "How can I get my kid to

---

[51] *The Six Pillars of Self-Esteem,* chapter 13, "Nurturing a Child's Self-Esteem."

do what I know is best?" the parents in Galt's Gulch think, "Be the hero you wish to see in your children."

And so we find a solution to the following complaints many people make to their therapists about their parents (and if you want, pause as you read each of these and check within to see if the statement is true for you): My parents never truly saw me . . . They didn't understand me, the real me . . . When I was telling them what I needed, they didn't listen to me . . . When I was telling them what I did *not* need, they didn't listen to me . . . They didn't take me seriously . . . They didn't treat my thoughts, my values, my self, with respect . . . And, worst of all, they worked so hard for my happiness,[52] when all I wanted, what I desperately needed, was to see theirs. To be inspired. To see the kind of life that is possible on this earth.[53]

My vision of the heroic parents of Galt's Gulch is the opposite of the above quote: they truly see their children — in this moment; they

---

[52] Note that most of the things parents make their kids do isn't even for their present happiness; it's for an imagined future happiness that may or may not come to pass.

[53] These complaints may be quoted or paraphrased from Nathaniel Branden. I have been unable to locate them in his books, but my original notes for this essay attribute them to him.

truly understand their children—their real children, not their imagined ones; they listen to what their children say they need, and they respect what their children say they don't need; they take their children seriously; they treat their children's thoughts, values, and selves with respect, and they inspire their children by how they live their lives.

Audre Lorde said, "The master's tools will never dismantle the master's house." Our current parenting tools are not the tools with which Galt's Gulch can be built. In fact, they are the tools that tear it down. Remember, the method is the message. When we live in the operating system of control, when we use the tools of control to fight for freedom and respect for individuals, we have already lost. When we fail to move out of that system psychologically, we have already lost.

Our outer world reflects our inner world. This goes two ways—right now our government reflects our households (benevolent dictatorships), and our households reflect our personal psychological status (the operating system of control). Our current outer world does, in fact, reflect our current inner world— there is no contradiction!

If we want our outer world to be one of freedom and respect, our households and our own personal psychology must reflect that.

Nathaniel Branden wrote, "Self-concept is destiny."[54] If we raise our children as people with ownership of their lives, they will take ownership of their lives. If we don't manipulate their feelings of pain and pleasure, reality will be their only master. If we don't use extrinsic motivators to control them, they will retain their intrinsic selves. If we don't use behaviorist tactics on them at all, behaviorist tactics will never be necessary. If we model and help them maintain self-awareness of their emotions, they will not lose valuable information through repression. If we relate to even our youngest children in respectful ways, they will relate to others in respectful ways, and we will live in a society more like Galt's Gulch.

Today, I think of Galt's Gulch as a psychological place. It's the dream, the place where it doesn't get any better. Today, when I picture the parents and children of Galt's Gulch, I picture relationships that are the dream, relationships that are safe havens of freedom, joy, and respect for both parent and child, relationships in which both parties feel, "It doesn't get better than this."

---

[54] *The Six Pillars of Self-Esteem*, chapter 1, "Self-Esteem: The Immune System of Consciousness."

Afterword

If you enjoyed this book, consider checking out my book of concrete examples of how I have raised my son, *City Family Farm Family*. Also consider checking out my YouTube channel (Roslyn Ross) and blog (RoslynRoss.Blogspot.com). At my blog you can also find a full bibliography of the books I read that helped me to come to these conclusions. I also review books on Goodreads.com.

If you wish to write me, please feel free. I enjoy reading emails from readers! However, be warned that I rarely respond. I apologize fot that. I wish it were not the case. My email address is RoslynRoss@gmail.com.

Acknowledgments

David Jay, Tom Garrett, and Wes Bertrand—thank you to for aiding in my examination of the contradictions.

Taylor Conant, Anne Stirling-Hastings, and Andrew Forrester—thank you for your comments on earlier drafts of this essay.

Alexander R. Cohen—thank you for your editing services.

Appendix: Recommended Reading

There are some great books out there that give more examples and more thorough explanations of how to have a respectful relationship with even the youngest of children. All of these books have minor inconsistencies with Objectivism and rarely (if ever) truly leave the operating system of control, but they remain the best out there, and I highly recommend them.

I have limited myself to the books I consider the most important in each category (after this book, my other book, *City Family Farm Family*, and my blog). I have listed the books in order of importance, starting with physical health, as our psychological health starts with our physical health.

If You Are Thinking About Having Kids

1. *The Baby Decision* by Merle Bombardieri
2. *Nutrition and Physical Degeneration* by Weston A. Price, *Nourishing Traditions* by Sally Fallon, or *Real Food for Mother and Baby* by Nina Planck
3. *Count Down: How Our Modern World is Threatening Sperm Counts, Altering Male and Female Reproductive Development…* by Shanna H. Swan
4. *It Starts with The Egg: How the Science of Egg Quality Can Help You…* by Rebecca Fett
5. *How to Raise a Healthy Child in Spite of Your Doctor* by Robert Mendelsohn
6. *The Price of Motherhood: Why the Most Important Job in the World Is Still the Least Valued* by Ann Crittenden
7. *Nonviolent Communication* by Marshall Rosenberg
8. *The Richest Man in Babylon* by George S. Clason
9. *12 Rules for Life: An Antidote to Chaos* by Jordan B. Peterson
10. *Pikler Bulletin #14* by Emmi Pikler from RIE.org

If You Are Expecting

1. *What's Right For Me?* By Sara Wickham
2. *Baby Catcher* by Peggy Vincent
3. *The Nourishing Traditions Book of Baby and Child Care* by Sally Fallon and Mary Enig
4. *How to Raise a Healthy Child in Spite of Your Doctor* by Robert Mendelsohn
5. *Vitamin K and the Newborn* by Sara Wickham
6. *Breastfeeding Made Simple* by Nancy Mohrbacher
7. *Pikler Bulletin #14* by Emmi Pikler from RIE.org
8. *Dear Parents: Caring for Infants with Respect* by Magda Gerber
9. *Nonviolent Communication* by Marshall Rosenberg
10. *The Art of Living Consciously* by Nathaniel Branden

Group B Strep Explained by Sara Wickham if you are diagnosed with Group B Strep

Inducing Labor: Making Informed Decisions by Sara Wickham if this is something you are considering

Anti-D Explained by Sara Wickham if you are Rh negative

If You Have a Baby

1. *How to Raise a Healthy Child in Spite of Your Doctor* by Robert Mendelsohn
2. *Pikler Bulletin #14* by Emmi Pikler from RIE.org
3. *The Nourishing Traditions Book of Baby and Child Care* by Sally Fallon and Mary Enig
4. *Close Your Mouth: Butekyo Clinic Handbook for Perfect Health* by Patrick McKeown
5. *Home Management plain and Simple* by Kim Brenneman
6. *Dear Parents: Caring for Infants with Respect* by Magda Gerber
7. *Tears and Tantrums* by Aletha Solter
8. *Baby-Led Weaning* by Gill Rapley and Tracey Murkett
9. *How to Get Your Kid to Eat... But Not Too Much* by Ellyn Satter
10. *The Vaccine Book: Making the Right Decision for Your Child* by Robert W. Sears, MD, FAAP

If You Have a Toddler

1. *How to Raise a Healthy Child in Spite of Your Doctor* by Robert Mendelsohn
2. *The Nourishing Traditions Book of Baby and Child Care* by Sally Fallon and Mary Enig
3. How *to Get Your Kid to Eat... But Not Too Much* by Ellyn Satter
4. *1,2,3... The Toddler Years* by Irene Van der Zande
5. *Tears and Tantrums* by Aletha Solter
6. *The Secret of Childhood* by Maria Montessori
7. *Connection Parenting* by Pam Leo
8. *Nonviolent Communication* by Marshall Rosenberg
9. *Escape from Childhood* by John Holt
10. *The Nurture Assumption: Why Children Turn Out the Way They Do* by Judith Rich Harris

*If you have not yet read Ayn Rand's "The Comprachicos," *Introduction to Objectivist Epistemology,* and *The Romantic Manifesto* this would be a good time to do so.

If You Have a Young Child (Ages 3-7)

1. *How to Raise a Healthy Child in Spite of Your Doctor* by Robert Mendelsohn
2. *Nutrition and Physical Degeneration* by Weston A. Price or *Nourishing Traditions* by Sally Fallon
3. How *to Get Your Kid to Eat... But Not Too Much* by Ellyn Satter
4. *The Child in the Family* or *The Secret of Childhood* by Maria Montessori
5. *Parent Effectiveness Training* by Thomas Gordon, *How to Talk so Kids Will Listen and Listen So Kids Will Talk* by Adele Faber and Elaine Mazlish, or *Nonviolent Communication* by Marshall Rosenberg
6. *Connection Parenting* by Pam Leo or *Parenting a Free Child* by Rue Kream
7. *Escape from Childhood* by John Holt
8. *The Nurture Assumption: Why Children Turn Out the Way They Do* by Judith Rich Harris
9. *The Underground History of American Education* by John Gatto, *The Deliberate Dumbing Down of American* by Charlotte Thomson Iserbyt

If You Have an Older Child, Teen, or Adult

1. *How to Raise a Healthy Child in Spite of Your Doctor* by Robert Mendelsohn
2. *Nutrition and Physical Degeneration* by Weston A. Price
3. *Nourishing Traditions* by Sally Fallon
4. *Escape from Childhood* by John Holt
5. *The Case Against Adolescence* by Robert Epstein
6. *Sex and Culture* by Joseph Daniel Unwin
7. *Connection Parenting* by Pam Leo, *How to Talk so Teens Will Listen and Listen So Teens Will Talk* by Adele Faber and Elaine Mazlish, or *Nonviolent Communication* by Marshall Rosenberg
8. *The Nurture Assumption: Why Children Turn Out the Way They Do* by Judith Rich Harris
9. *The Underground History of American Education* by John Gatto or *The Deliberate Dumbing Down of America* by Charlotte Thomson Iserbyt
10. *Parenting a Free Child* by Rue Kream

The Best Food for Thought

1. *The Nurture Assumption: Why Children Turn Out the Way They Do* by Judith Rich Harris
2. *To Train Up a Child: Child Training for the 21st Century* by Michael Pearl and Debi Pearl
3. *Hold on to Your Kids* by Gordon Neufeld and Gabor Maté MD
4. *Sex and Culture* by Joseph Daniel Unwin
5. *Skip College* by Connor Boyack
6. *The Selfish Gene* by Richard Dawkins
7. *Human Diversity: The Biology of Gender, Race, and Class* by Charles Murray
8. *Family Fortunes* by Bill Bonner
9. *Indiviualism and Collectivism* by Harry C Triandis
10. *Mother Nature: Maternal Instincts and How They Shape the Human Species* by sasrah Hrdy

Made in United States
Troutdale, OR
03/14/2024